This book belongs to

....

THE MYSTERIES OF MIGRATION

Geeta Dharmarajan

Art by Sarasija Subramanian

KATHA

"Help!" I shout, looking at the sky. "A bird attack!"

“Silly!” says my friend, Malar. “They are flamingos. They come to India in winters.”

Birds. Fishes. Mammals.
Insects. Reptiles.
Guess one amazing thing
most of them do?

They move thousands of miles every year, to return to where they were born. And then they move back again! This is called migration. They move from cold homes in the north to the warm south, and back again.

Do they migrate because of cold weather? Or in search of food? And why do they always return to their cold homes?

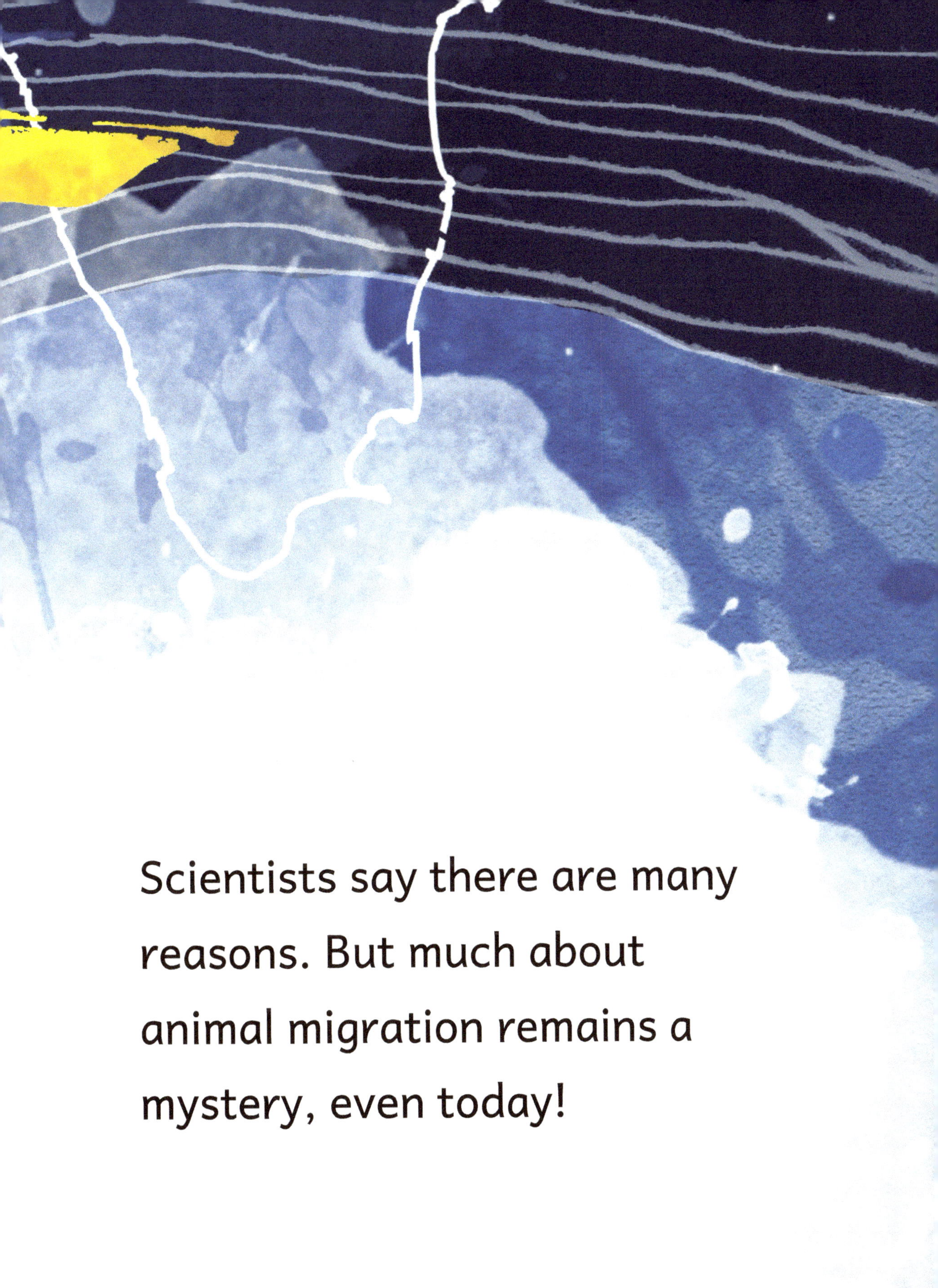

Scientists say there are many reasons. But much about animal migration remains a mystery, even today!

The Vanishing Trick

Adult green turtles of Brazil go all of 1,400 miles to Ascension Island, a speck in the vast Atlantic, to lay their eggs.

One miss and they'll be in Africa! Yet, no turtle has been seen there!

Scientists believe that a turtle's eyesight is not good enough for it to steer by the stars.

So do they use the sun's rays as clues? Or the 'smell' of Ascension Island?

Here's another mystery! Baby green turtles leave Ascension Island for Brazil when a few weeks old. Yet, no turtle less than a year has been spotted anywhere in the world! Where do these baby turtles go? Perhaps we'll know one day!

Do you know that five species of turtles are known to inhabit the Indian coastline, and three of their biggest nesting beaches are in Odisha?

A Whale of a Trip!

BRRR ...! It's so cold in the waters of the Polar Regions. No place for baby whales to be born — or for yearlings.

And the food's not easy to get!
So these gigantic mammals,
the humpback whales, move
to warmer waters.

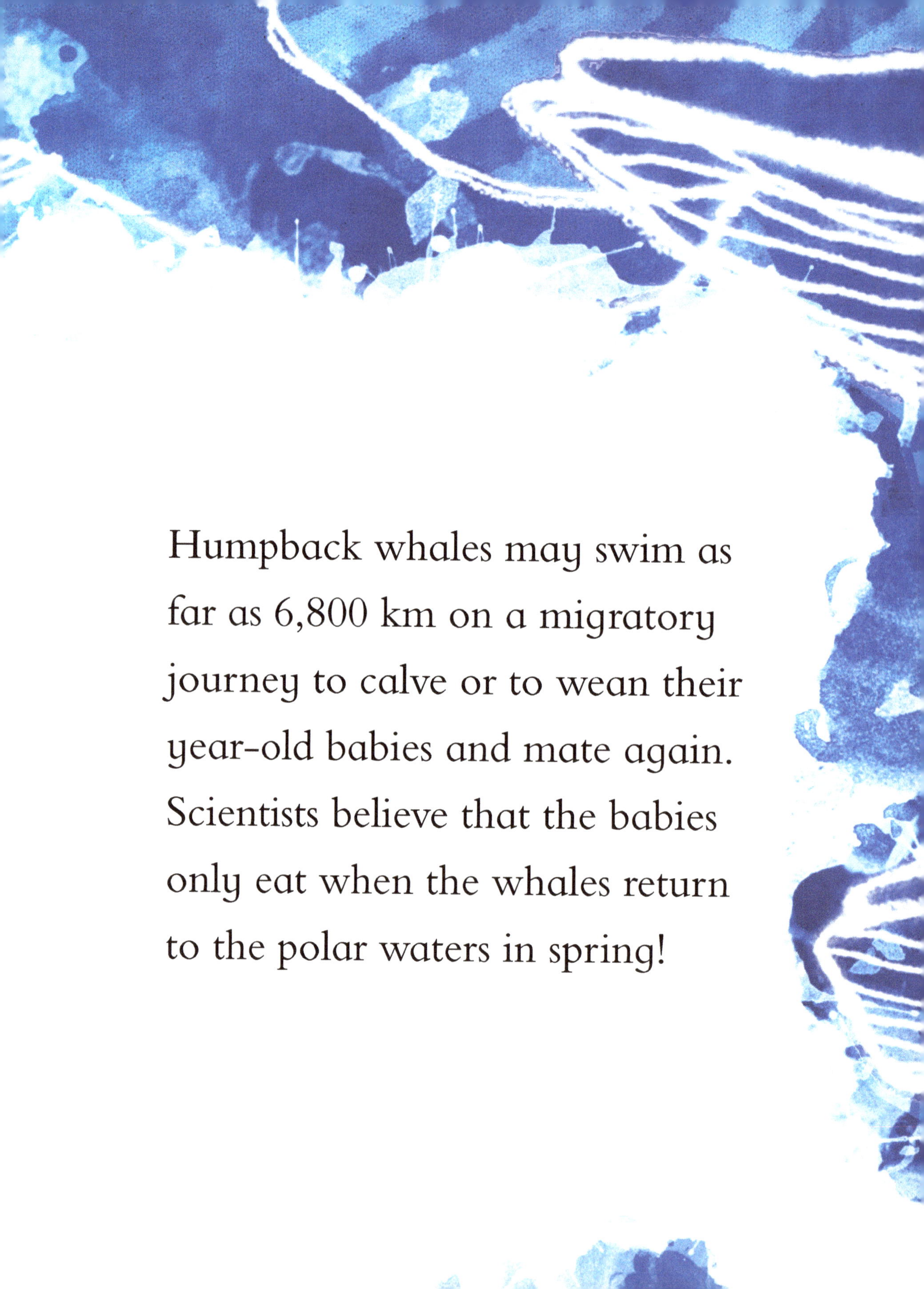

Humpback whales may swim as far as 6,800 km on a migratory journey to calve or to wean their year-old babies and mate again. Scientists believe that the babies only eat when the whales return to the polar waters in spring!

Off We Go – and Back!

Some birds that are born in warm places migrate to cold places in search of food. And when it gets too cold, they come back home to warm places.

Many of these birds fly hours by day while migrating. Many do not eat while migrating. How do they have the energy to fly on and on and on?

Scientists say that they store up fat and use it as fuel.

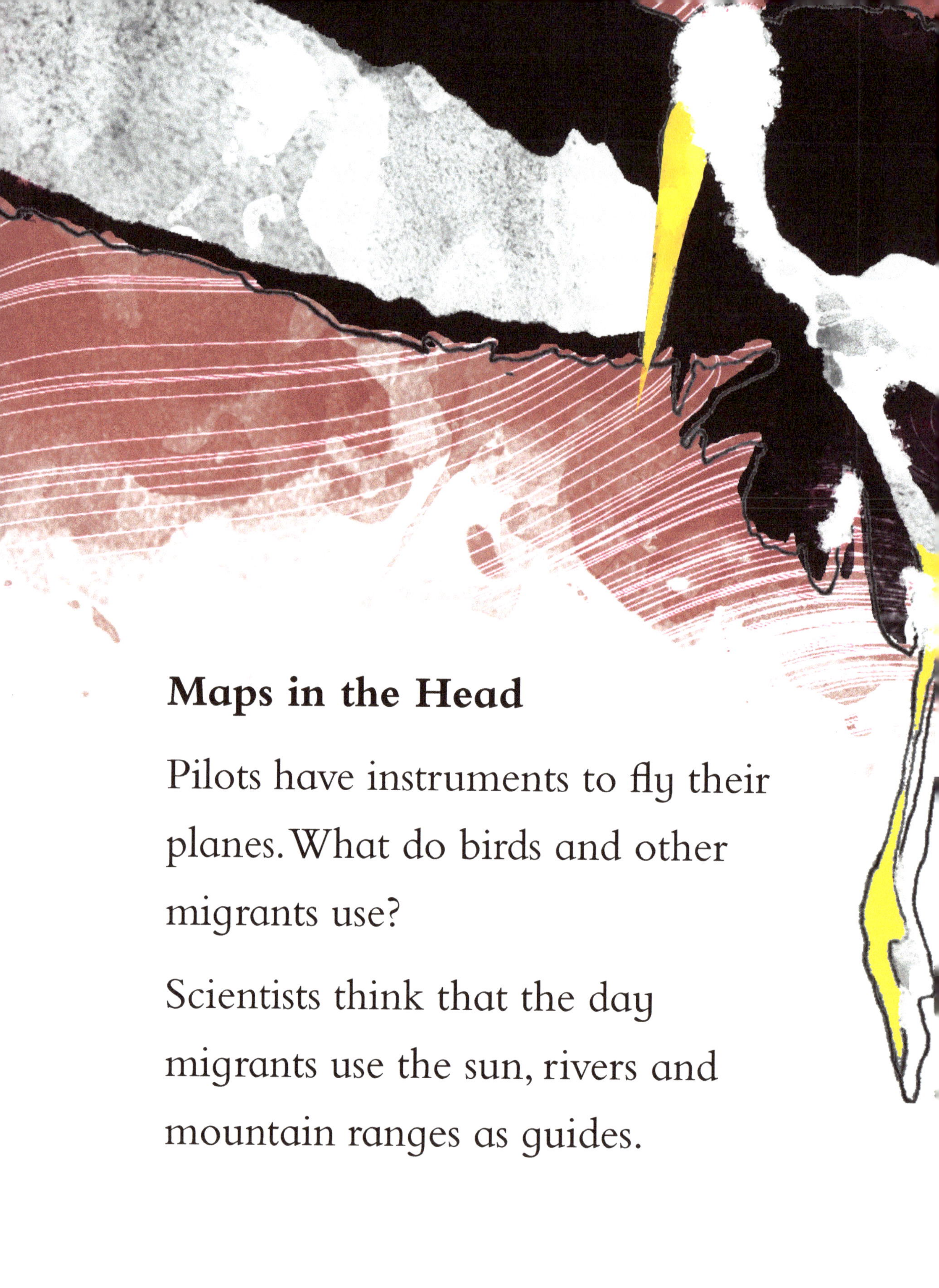

Maps in the Head

Pilots have instruments to fly their planes. What do birds and other migrants use?

Scientists think that the day migrants use the sun, rivers and mountain ranges as guides.

The night fliers probably use the stars, or orient themselves by the moon, the wind, the earth's magnetic field – helped by some kind of internal 'biological clock'!

Sailing on the Wind

FLAP ... GL ... I ... DE! The baby storks are off to their winter homes in Africa and India! The adults follow later.

So how do the babies know how or where to go? Or that they should use the hot-air currents (as do many other long-distance migrants) to carry them, so that they save energy?

How do storks know when to leave? Scientists believe that shortening days and changes within a bird's body tell it when to move!

The storks time it exactly right every year. Come spring, they are off — back to their northern homes.

No one knows how they fly back to the very same nests year after year, almost on the same date too!

Swiftly Fly Butterfly

You wouldn't travel hundreds of miles to sleep, would you? But the Monarch butterflies do just that! Come autumn and they fly from Canada and the northern states of America to as far south as Mexico!

There they cling half-sleepily
to thousands of trees.

Though a hundred of
these butterflies weigh
just an ounce, thousands
of them resting can bend
heavy branches!

Year after year new generations of Monarch butterflies find the same trees to sleep on — yet none of them has made the trip before.

A Monarch butterfly lives just ten months and makes only one migratory trip!

Around March, Monarch butterflies fly north again.

Millions on the Move

Rub your eyes and look again! A million or more animals are on the move! Impossible? Just visit Serengeti, East Africa, at migration time.

Wildebeests (say, wil-duh-beasts), zebras and gazelles are off on an 800-mile trek, following pathways worn out by millions of hoots over thousands of years.

These animals escape not from cold, but from droughts. They leave long before the water has dried up, returning only when the rains green the grasslands in December. How do they know when to move?

Maybe one day you will be the scientist who discovers more about the mysteries of migration!

Think

Are there any birds that come to your neighbourhood or an area such as a lake or a river near your home at a particular time of the year? Do you know their names?

Ask

Birds and animals are able to migrate freely, but what about human beings? Can we also migrate freely? What helps or prevents free-flowing human migration? Do lands, seas and skies have borders?

Discuss

If you had a choice to migrate every year, where would you like to migrate?

Act

Migration is an inspiring natural phenomenon. Every year thousands of birds fly down to India to the wetlands in Rajasthan, Odisha, Andhra Pradesh and Gujarat. But like in other parts of the world, these birds are facing a lot of challenges like loss of habitat and climate change. Some of these birds are becoming endangered.

How do you think we can help? Here are some things to start you off!

- Throw garbage in the dustbin.
- Grow plants that belong to your region.
- Don't use pesticides.
- Don't buy furniture made from rainforests.
- Learn more about the endangered species in your area and spread awareness.

OUR ONLY HOME . CARE & SHARE

Geeta Dharmarajan loves writing for children. She received the Padma Shri in 2012 for her work in literature and education.

Sarasija Subramanian is a photographer and design enthusiast. She is an art student with an itch to pen things down.

KATHA

Katha is a globally recognised non-profit organization (www.katha.org) that has been working in the literacy to literature continuum since 1988. Our nearly 30 years of experience is in publishing and education for children in poverty.

"An educational jewel in India's crown." **— Naoyuki Shinohara, Deputy Managing Director, IMF**

"Katha stands as an exemplar for all the creative projects around the world that grapple with ordinary and dramatic misery in cities." **— Charles Landry, *The Art of City Making***

"Katha has a real soft corner for kids. Which is why it ... create[s] such gorgeous picture books for children." **— Time Out**

"Katha's work is driven by the idea that children can bring change to their communities that is sustainable and real, just as the children do in [their books.]" **— Papertigers**

First published by Katha, 2017

A3, Sarvodaya Enclave, Sri Aurobindo Marg, New Delhi 110 017
Phone: 91-11 4141 6600 . 4141 6610 . Fax: 91-11 2651 4373
E-mail: editors@katha.org, Website: www.katha.org

Our Mission: Every child reading well and for fun!
I Love Reading Library is a unique series of books that brings new/diffident readers into sustainable learning. With high-quality content and design to match the learning needs of children at different reading levels, it brings the best of India's 2000 years of literary heritage. Based on StoryPedagogy devised by Geeta Dharmarajan, these books help increase young readers' ability to understand BIG ideas for change and help them build a kinder, more sustainable world.

ISBN 978-93-82454-51-9

Ten per cent of sales proceeds from this book will support the quality education of children studying in Katha Schools.
Katha regularly plants trees to replace the wood used in the making of its books.

www.ingramcontent.com/pod-product-compliance
Ingram Content Group UK Ltd.
Pitfield, Milton Keynes, MK11 3LW, UK
UKHW062005290726
14090UKWH00022B/1405